When we first discussed setting the sails on this series, the storms we were about to weather never occurred to us. We didn't stop to ponder the fact that we were trying to release an untried property into a market that might not want it. We never considered that not many people might be interested in such a story. No thought was given to the idea that not many publishers might have an interest in it either.

Well, once we weighed anchor and began our voyage, we started considering all these things. Just as a child's imagination can dash their make-believe ships on the rocky shores of fear, we found ourselves staring at the specter of what we'd created like a captain piloting his vessel into obviously troubled waters.

Were we about to have our hopes and dreams broadsided by the cruel realities of publishing in today's market? Were we preparing to embark on a fool's errand across a horizon from which no one had ever returned?

This, and many other fears, danced through our heads, until, like an errant ship pulled by an unrelenting tide, we found ourselves drawn into the creation of this mythos. We began to embrace our heroes, empathize with our young protagonist and come to the realization that by learning to be brave, we too, could overcome the frightening, endure the uncertainty and guide our craft onward to calm waters and blue skies.

Thank you for picking up our book. We hope you enjoy reading it as much as we enjoyed creating it.

-Mike Bullock & Jack Lawrence

JACK

Everything was perfect. Robert and Gary were right down the street. We just finished hooking up my treehouse...we could play football whenever we wanted.
I had GRANDMA right next door...
Now, ever since Mom took that CRUMMY new job and I found out we have to MOVE, everything is all MESSED up.
We won't get to HANG in my tree house...we won't be able to play football...
And I won't get to see Grandma hardly EVER...
WHY did Mom have to go and get a NEW job? Her old job was fine, but NOOOO she had to have a NEW one. Why does she need to be on a 'fast track' anyway? I thought she was already independent without Dad around anymore...
I'm gonna miss out on the field trip to the Halloween Park now, too. I'll never get Buddy to stop teasing me if I don't go through that Haunted House.
He says I'm chicken...so what if I wouldn't go in last year...
I just didn't want to...

Grandma always tells me to CONFRONT my fears. Going into that Haunted House would show everyone I'm not scared of nuthin!
Grandma says they have Beasties there, though. Mom never BELIEVED in Beasties, she thinks they're just another one of Grandma's CRAZY stories.
But I KNOW they're there.
I've seen them. I HEAR them at night. I know that noise in my closet isn't a mouse like Mom says, it's a BEASTIE!
Who's going to scare the Beasties away in stupid ol' Greenville?
Without Grandma to read to me and make sure I'm safe, how will I be able to sleep? I bet the Beasties will GET me!
I wonder if they know I'm leaving. I'll bet they do. I'll bet they're WATCHING me...
...right now.
AHHH!

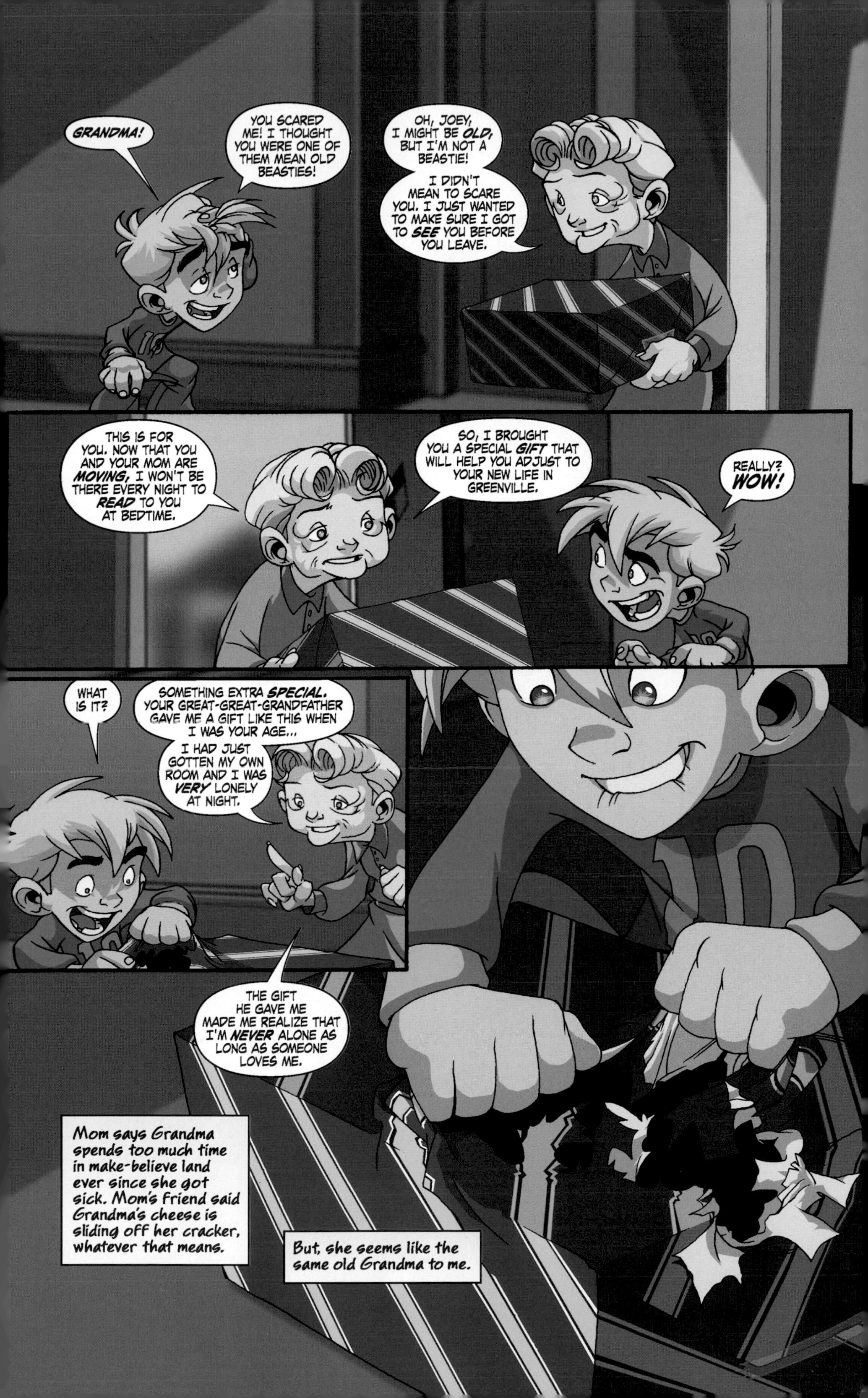
GRANDMA!
YOU SCARED ME! I THOUGHT YOU WERE ONE OF THEM MEAN OLD BEASTIES!
OH, JOEY, I MIGHT BE OLD, BUT I'M NOT A BEASTIE!
I DIDN'T MEAN TO SCARE YOU. I JUST WANTED TO MAKE SURE I GOT TO SEE YOU BEFORE YOU LEAVE.
THIS IS FOR YOU. NOW THAT YOU AND YOUR MOM ARE MOVING, I WON'T BE THERE EVERY NIGHT TO READ TO YOU AT BEDTIME.
SO, I BROUGHT YOU A SPECIAL GIFT THAT WILL HELP YOU ADJUST TO YOUR NEW LIFE IN GREENVILLE.
REALLY? WOW!
WHAT IS IT?
SOMETHING EXTRA SPECIAL. YOUR GREAT-GREAT-GRANDFATHER GAVE ME A GIFT LIKE THIS WHEN I WAS YOUR AGE...
I HAD JUST GOTTEN MY OWN ROOM AND I WAS VERY LONELY AT NIGHT.
THE GIFT HE GAVE ME MADE ME REALIZE THAT I'M NEVER ALONE AS LONG AS SOMEONE LOVES ME.
Mom says Grandma spends too much time in make-believe land ever since she got sick. Mom's friend said Grandma's cheese is sliding off her cracker, whatever that means.
But, she seems like the same old Grandma to me.

WHOA...
...THIS IS AWESOME, GRANDMA!
No matter what mom thinks, Grandma still gets me the BEST presents! She knows how much I LOVE tigers!
"THE NIGHT PRIDE: PROTECTORS OF THE INNOCENT."
"THE NIGHT PRIDE IS AN ORDER OF FOUR, NEVER LESS, NEVER MORE."
Night Pride
Protectors of the innocent
Pallo
Leader of the Pack
Venus
Guardian of the Pride

"THERE'S MINERVA...
"...VENUS...
"...PALLO...
"...AND ARES."
THANK YOU, GRANDMA! I LOVE THEM!
I KNEW YOU WOULD MISS ALL YOUR FRIENDS HERE WHEN YOU MOVED, SO I THOUGHT THESE STUFFED ANIMALS MIGHT KEEP YOU COMPANY.
THESE ARE THE NIGHT PRIDE, JOEY, YOUR NEW FRIENDS.
NOW WHENEVER YOU FEEL LIKE YOU'RE ALL ALONE, JUST REMEMBER YOU HAVE THESE FOUR NEW COMPANIONS.
THEY'LL BE YOUR FRIENDS FROM NOW UNTIL YOU GET OLD LIKE ME.
the Night Pride
Protectors of the innocent
ares
warrior of the night
the night pride is an order of four. never less. never more.

LONE RIDER MOVING
This house is CREEPY, I feel like someone is watching me...I hope this place isn't HAUNTED...
That would be just my luck, we leave a PERFECTLY good house and move into a haunted one!
REMEMBER WHAT GRANDMA SAID, I HAVE FOUR NEW FRIENDS AND I NEED TO BE BRAVE--
BOOM
AHHHH!
SORRY, I DROPPED A BOX.
HAVE YOU GOT ALL YOUR THINGS UNPACKED YET?
I START WORK TOMORROW AND WON'T HAVE TIME TO HELP YOU WITH MUCH UNTIL I GET HOME, SO IF YOU NEED ANY HELP MOVING THINGS AROUND, TELL ME NOW.
I'M FINE, MOM, I'LL FINISH UNPACKING TOMORROW...
PROMISE.
OKAY, DON'T STAY UP TOO LATE.

"A CHILD'S INSTINCTUAL NEED FOR THE COMFORT OF A STUFFED ANIMAL IS ROOTED IN A REALITY LONG FORGOTTEN BY THE ADULT WORLD.
"THE HIDDEN TRUTH IS THAT THESE COMPANIONS HAVE BEEN DEFENDING CHILDREN SINCE THE DAWN OF TIME."
COOOOL.
"SET THE NIGHT PRIDE AROUND YOUR BED, ONE AT EACH CORNER, AND GO TO SLEEP KNOWING THESE GUARDIANS WILL PROTECT YOU THROUGH THE NIGHT."
MINERVA, HUNTRESS OF THE SHADOWS... COOL!
VENUS, GUARDIAN OF THE PRIDE...
PALLO, LEADER OF THE PACK... SUH-LICK!
ARES, WARRIOR OF THE NIGHT...HE IS DEFINITELY MY FAVORITE!
"SET THE NIGHT PRIDE AROUND YOUR BED...
"... ONE AT EACH CORNER..."

"'...AND GO TO SLEEP KNOWING THEY WILL PROTECT YOU THROUGH THE NIGHT.'"
COME ON, MUMBLER, THE KID'S ASLEEP. IF WE DON'T GET HIM NOW, GROK WILL EAT YOU FOR DINNER.
WHY WOULD HE EAT ME AND NOT YOU? YOU'RE FAT AND RIPE. I THINK HE'D RATHER EAT YOU, MAYBE WITH SOME FRIES AND KETCHUP...
SHUT UP!
OK, LET'S GET HIM BEFORE HE WAKES UP!
GRRRR...

HUH?
WHUZZAT?
S'NOTHIN'.
SLAM

HUH?
WHAT ARE YOU DOING OVER THERE, PALLO... HOW DID THE CLOSET DOOR GET SHUT?
YAAAWN
MUST HAVE BEEN THE WIND...
...OR MAYBE I'M JUST...
...DREAMING...

...HAD THE WEIRDEST DREAM, GRANDMA!
THE NIGHT PRIDE CHASED OFF THE BEASTIES WHILE I WAS SLEEPING, JUST LIKE YOU SAID THEY WOULD!
TIGERMAN FLAKES
I TOLD YOU THEY'D PROTECT YOU.
IT'S WHAT THEY'VE BEEN DOING FOR A LONG, LONG TIME.
I THINK IT MIGHT JUST BE A GOOD THING THAT YOU DON'T HAVE YOUR SILLY OLD GRANDMA AROUND ALL THE TIME ANYMORE. YOUR FEARS ARE JUST A PART OF YOUR IMAGINATION, IT'S TIME YOU STARTED USING THAT IMAGINATION TO BE BRAVE INSTEAD OF SCARED.
I'LL TRY, GRANDMA! JUST YOU WAIT AND SEE, WITH THESE CATS HELPING ME, I CAN OVERCOME ANY BEASTIE THERE IS!
ARES SAT WITH ME WHILE I PLAYED VIDEO GAMES THIS MORNING. I THINK HE'S GOOD LUCK. IF I CAN BEAT THE BLARGIAN BOSS ON LEVEL 12, I CAN BEAT ANYTHING!
THAT'S MY JOSEPH. WHAT A FINE YOUNG MAN YOU'RE TURNING OUT TO BE.
I MISS YOU, GRANDMA. I MISS MY FRIENDS, TOO...
I KNOW YOU DO, JOSEPH. BUT YOU'LL MAKE NEW FRIENDS SOON ENOUGH.
NOW YOU NEED TO STOP DWELLING ON THE SAD THINGS. LET ME TELL YOU A STORY NOW, THE ONE YOUR MOTHER ALWAYS SAYS I'M CRAZY FOR TELLING, BUT I SWEAR IT'S TRUE.

STUFFED ANIMAL KINGDOM
STUFFED ANIMAL KINGDOM
WHEN I WAS A LITTLE GIRL, I WAS VERY AFRAID OF THE DARK... VERY AFRAID.
"BUT MY GRANDFATHER TOOK ME TO A PLACE WHERE HE GOT ME A VERY SPECIAL PRESENT THAT WOULD KEEP ME SAFE AT NIGHT.
"HE TOLD ME A DEAR FRIEND OF HIS, WHOSE LIFE HE HAD SAVED IN THE GREAT WAR, HAD GIVEN HIM THIS BEAR AS A GIFT FOR ME.
STUFFED ANIMAL KINGDOM bear
"AND HE TOLD ME OF THE MAGIC INSTILLED IN THESE SPECIAL ANIMALS. TO MOST ADULTS, THEY'RE JUST ORDINARY STUFFED ANIMALS.
"BUT TO THOSE WHO STILL BELIEVE IN MAGIC, THEY'RE SO MUCH MORE THAN ORDINARY.

"THESE ANIMALS COME IN ALL SHAPES AND SIZES. BIG ONES, TALL ONES, LARGE ONES, SMALL ONES.
"EACH ONE IS BLESSED WITH LIFE FROM THEIR MAKER.
" A LIFE THAT IS PLEDGED TO DEFEND CHILDREN FROM THE THINGS THAT GO BUMP IN THE NIGHT."
EVERY NIGHT, ALWAYS REMEMBER...

BE BRAVE, LITTLE LION!
WE'RE GOING TO EAT YOUR LITTLE FRIEND, TIGER-MAN, AND THERE'S NOTHING YOU CAN DO ABOUT IT!
UNTIE MY SIDE KICK, SQUID MARK! YOUR VILE VILLAINY WILL NOT OVERSHADOW THE RIGHT HAND OF JUSTICE!
LOOK OUT, TIGER-MAN!
ONLY THE ROCK OCTOPUS COULD SNEAK UP ON TIGER-MAN! NOW WE'LL SEE HOW BRAVE YOU REALLY ARE...
EEEEP!
OHMYGODWHATISTHAT?
I HAVE TO BE BRAVE. I HAVE TO BE BRAVE.
TIGER-MAN WOULD BE BRAVE. IF HE CAN DO IT, SO CAN I.

W-WHAT THE--
I MUST BE DREAMING! THIS CAN'T BE HAPPENING!

W-W-WHAT IS THAT?
WE'RE GETTIN' THAT KID, PALLO, AND YOU CAN'T STOP US!
JOEY IS UNDER OUR PROTECTION, GRUMBLE. YOU AND MUMBLER BETTER FIND ANOTHER WAY TO SPEND YOUR NIGHTS.
=MUMBLE= STUPID STUFFED ANIMAL MILITIA =MUMBLE MUMBLE=
GRRRRRR
"JOEY IS UNDER OUR PROTECTION..." I'M JOEY... THOSE LOOK LIKE MY STUFFED ANIMALS! DO THEY MEAN ME?

AAAA!
RAKRRR
KEEP 'EM BUSY, MUMBLER...
I'LL GET THE KID!
ARES, HE'S GOING FOR JOEY!
YOU HAVE TO STOP HIM! I CAN HANDLE MUMBLER!
I'M ON IT!
GET BACK HERE, BEASTIE!
RAKRRR

OOOF!
WHERE DO YOU THINK *YOU'RE* GOING, BEASTIE!
WHAMM
≈GULP≈ MOM?
BAMM

CRAAASH
ROARRRRR!
BAMM

OUT OF MY WAY, HAIRBALL!
OOOF!
I'LL GET THIS KID YET!
RRRRR! NOW YOU MADE ME MAD! GET BACK HERE, YOU MOLDY GRAPE!
OHMANOHMANOHMANOHMAN
SHRIPP

I GOT YOU NOW, KID!
GET AWAY FROM HIM!
ROARRR
AHHHH!
OOOF!
SHHHLMP

To Be Continued

"Alter Egos"
By
Andy Runton

JACK

AAAHHHH!
HELP MEEEEEE!
GET OFF ME, YOU OVERGROWN RODENT!
NOT SO TOUGH WHEN YOU AREN'T FIGHTING CHILDREN, ARE YOU, MUMBLER?
URRRRK! KILL... YOU... GRRRK!... PALLO!

OWW!
GAHHH!
OOOFF!
RROOAARR!
AHHHCCCK
COME ON, MINERVA, IT'S DINNER TIME!
REEEAAAAR!
GAH! MORE OF THEM! MAKE FOR THE WOODS, MUMBLER!
I THINK I HAVE SOME WEEDS STUCK IN MY TEETH...
FORGET THE DENTAL HYGIENE AND RUN!
VENUS! LET THEM GO, WE CAN HUNT LATER!
WELCOME TO THE WAR, JOEY. YOU'VE JUST BEEN INJURED IN COMBAT FOR THE FIRST TIME.
WHAT DO YOU MEAN? I WASN'T SHOT.
NO, BUT LOOK AT THAT SCRAPE ON YOUR KNEE!
YOU WERE HELPING ME FIGHT OFF GRUMBLE, YA KNOW. ONE THING YOU LEARN OVER THE YEAR THOSE BEASTIES CAN GET NASTY.
YA KNOW YOU LOOK AN AWFUL LOT LIKE THE STUFFED ANIMALS MY GRANDMA GAVE ME...ARE YOU ARES?
YEP, THE ONE AND ONLY!

NOOOO WAAAY, GRANDMA SAID YOU WERE MAGIC. MAYBE HER CHEESE HASN'T SLID OFF HER CRACKER.
ANYONE KNOW WHAT THAT MEANS?
W-WHERE ARE WE...? I NEED TO GO HOME.
AND WHAT'S A CRACKER?
YOU'RE IN THE STUFFED ANIMAL KINGDOM. AND WE ARE HOME--
...OH WAIT, YOU MEAN YOUR HOME...WE'LL GET YOU HOME... NO PROBLEM.
HEY, PALLO... HOW DO WE GET HIM HOME?
WE'VE NEVER HAD A REAL CHILD HERE IN THE KINGDOM.
ANY IDEAS?
WE CAN'T OPEN A TREE PORTAL WITHOUT A SCROLL, AND LITTLE BIRDIE WON'T BE BY HERE FOR SOME TIME.
WE MUST GO SEE THE KING.
KING? I DON'T WANNA SEE A KING, I WANNA SEE MY GRANDMA.
My knee stings a bit, don't remember ever feeling PAIN in a dream. They DO look just like the Night Pride... maybe Grandma was right...
I WANNA GO HOME.
KING BEAR WILL HELP US GET YOU HOME. THAT'S WHY WE NEED TO GO TO THE CASTLE.
IT'LL BE GOOD TO SEE MY OLD FRIEND AGAIN AFTER ALL THIS TIME.
FOLLOW US, LITTLE ONE. IT ISN'T TOO FAR.
OKAY, I GUESS... IF THAT'S THE ONLY WAY TO GET HOME... THERE AREN'T ANY MORE BEASTIES HERE ARE THERE?
THEY WOULDN'T DARE. THE GROVE IS THE CLOSEST THEY'LL COME TO KING BEAR AND HIS GUARDSMAN.
WELL, IF I AM DREAMING, I'LL WAKE UP SOON AND I DON'T WANT TO JUST SIT HERE BEING BORED UNTIL THEN.
IF I'M NOT DREAMING I REALLY DON'T WANT TO SIT HERE ALONE. ALL RIGHT, LET'S G--
B-B-B-BEAR!
BEAR?!
DID YOU SAY BEAR!?!

NUH-UH! I DON'T WANNA MEET A BEAR! BEARS EAT LITTLE KIDS LIKE ME! NO WAY!
DON'T WORRY. HE MIGHT LOOK BIG AND MEAN, BUT WHEN YOU GET TO KNOW HIM, HE'S JUST A BIG OLD TEDDY BEAR.
BE BRAVE, LITTLE LION. KING BEAR WANTS TO PROTECT YOU.
WAITAMINUTE...
...WHAT DID YOU JUST SAY?
"KING BEAR WANTS TO PROTECT YOU?"
NO, THE OTHER THING...BEFORE THAT...
"BE BRAVE, LITTLE LION?"
WHERE DID YOU GET THAT FROM? TIGER-MAN SAYS THAT!
TIGER-MAN? WHAT'S A TIGER-MAN?
ONLY THE GREATEST SUPER-HERO WHO EVER LIVED! YOU EVEN KINDA LOOK LIKE HIM.
DID YOU HEAR THAT, LADIES? I'M A SUPER HERO!

HEH.
YEAH, WHATEVER... SUPER-HERO... PFFT, THAT'LL HAPPEN.
OKAY, SUPER-HERO, YOU GET TO CARRY HIM.
ALL RIGHT, KID, JUMP ON THE TIGER-MAN EXPRESS. NEXT STOP, KING BEAR'S THRONE ROOM.
THANKS ARES, I NEVER GOT TO RIDE A REAL, LIVE TIGER BEFORE. WAIT UNTIL GRANDMA HEARS ABOU--
AAAH!
YA MIGHT WANNA HANG ON.
HANG ON. GOTCHA. MAN, I WANNA GO HOME...

YOU DON'T NEED TO HANG ON SO TIGHT. RELAX A LITTLE, ENJOY THE RIDE.
SO, HOW CAN YOU BE MY STUFFED ANIMALS AND BE REAL LIVE CATS AT THE SAME TIME?
WE CAN'T, ISN'T THAT OBVIOUS?
MINERVA, STOP BEING SO CATTY.
DON'T MIND MINERVA, SHE THINKS SARCASM IS A SPORTING EVENT.
DOESN'T SARCASM INVOLVE CHEESE AND CRACKERS?
WE'VE NEVER QUESTIONED OUR SHAPE CHANGING ANY MORE THAN YOU QUESTION WHY YOU HEAL. IT'S JUST HOW OUR MAKER WANTS US TO BE...
WELL...

"...WHO IS YOUR MAKER?"
IT'S GOOD YOU'VE DECIDED ON A NEW CAREER, COURTNEY, BUT WHAT HAPPENED TO FOLLOWING IN MY FOOTSTEPS?
DAD, DID YOU KNOW THAT THERE ARE OVER TWO HUNDRED BONES IN THE HUMAN BODY?
AND IF IT WASN'T FOR THOSE BONES, WE'D BE SOFT AND SQUISHY. YOU EVER BREAK A BONE?
YES, A LONG TIME AGO. WHEN I WAS A LITTLE BOY, NOT MUCH OLDER THAN YOU ARE NOW, I BROKE MY ARM PLAYING WAR. MY FRIENDS AND I ALL WANTED TO BE SOLDIERS, MORE THAN ANYTHING IN THE WORLD.
WE HAD STICKS FOR GUNS, AND BUSHES FOR FORTS. WE MARCHED AND WE FOUGHT BATTLES AND TOOK TURNS PRETENDING TO DIE. IT WOULD GO ON ALL DAY, UNTIL OUR MOTHERS PUT DINNER ON THE TABLE AND CALLED US HOME.
THEN...WHEN I WAS OLDER, I TOLD YOUR GRANDFATHER I WAS GOING TO BE A SOLDIER. HE BEGGED ME NOT TO GO. HE SAID "ABNER, YOU DON'T KNOW WHAT WAR IS AND TRUST ME, YOU DON'T WANT TO FIND OUT."
BUT I THOUGHT I KNEW BEST SO I WENT...
...AND FOUND OUT THAT NO ONE CALLED YOU IN FOR DINNER AT THE END OF THE DAY. AND NOT VERY MANY OF US WENT HOME AT ALL.
COULD YOU MAKE A BEAR WITH BONES IN HIM?

YOU THINK OUR ANIMALS NEED BONES? IS THAT WHY YOU HAD A CHANGE OF HEART?
WHAT WAS IT LIKE?
WHAT WAS WHAT LIKE?
THE WAR... ISN'T WAR SUPPOSED TO BE FUN? IF IT ISN'T, WHY WOULD THE BOYS PLAY IT ALL THE TIME?
WAR IS AWFUL, YOUNG LADY. UNFORTUNATELY, LITTLE BOYS NEVER LEARN...
IS THAT WHY YOU STOPPED PLAYING WAR AND STARTED WORKING WITH GRANDPA?
YES, COURTNEY, IT IS...

LET ME ASK YOU A QUESTION NOW.
OKAY. IS IT ABOUT BONES?
WHY DO YOU WANT TO BE A DOCTOR?
I GUESS I JUST WANT TO MAKE PEOPLE FEEL BETTER.
WELCOME, LITTLE LION...

...TO THE CRYSTAL CASTLE.
WHOOOOOOAAAAA!

HALT!
WHERE ARE YOU GOING WITH THIS BOY?
TO SEE THE KING.
TAKE A HUMAN BEFORE THE KING? PREPOSTEROUS!
WHERE DID YOU FIND THIS CHILD?
THEY, UH, LOOK LIKE THE NIGHT PRIDE...
OUR MISSION TO PROTECT HIM TOOK AN UNEXPECTED TURN.
WHAT'S GOING ON HERE?
MAJOR ORSON! THESE CATS ARE ATTEMPTING TO BRING A CHILD INTO THE GREAT HALL!
THESE AREN'T JUST CATS, THIS IS COMMANDER PALLO AND HIS PRIDE. STEP ASIDE AND LET THEM PASS.
THE COMMANDER PALLO?...
I TOLD YOU IT WAS THE NIGHT PRIDE...

SIR, WE HAD NO IDEA. WE MEANT NO OFFENSE!
NEVER APOLOGIZE FOR DOING YOUR DUTY, CORPORAL.
KEEP THE CASTLE SAFE, WORRY ABOUT HURT FEELINGS LATER.
...GROK AND HIS CRONIES...
...ARE GETTING MORE DARING...
...THEY HAVE GAINED ACCESS?
...SURELY, THE KING WILL HAVE THOUGHT...
...ONLY TRAVELS WITH GLOOM AND DOOM AT HIS SIDE...
LITTLE BIRDIE AND HIS PATROL BROUGHT US NEWS OF YOUR SITUATION.
THEY WERE RETURNING FROM THEIR RECON MISSION WHEN ARES AND THE CHILD FELL THROUGH THE PORTAL.
IT CAME AS QUITE THE SURPRISE TO US, MAJOR ORSON.
THAT'S THE CLOSEST GRUMBLE AND MUMBLER HAVE EVER COME TO GETTING JOEY.
IT WAS VERY FORTUNATE KING BEAR SENT US WHEN HE DID.
WOW!
LOOK AT THIS PLACE!
SO THE KING KNOWS THAT JOEY IS HERE?
YES, VENUS. HE ANTICIPATED THIS OUTCOME.
WISH HE WOULDA TOLD US...
HE HAD NO WAY TO PREPARE US FOR EVERY EVENTUALITY, MINERVA.

CAN I GO HOME NOW? MY GRANDMA IS GOING TO BE REALLY WORRIED ABOUT ME...
WE HAVE TO SEE THE KING FIRST, HE'LL KNOW HOW TO GET YOU HOME, LITTLE LION. COME... THIS WAY.
I DON'T WANNA GO DOWN THERE... IT'S SCARY...
THERE IS NOTHING TO FEAR HERE, LITTLE LION. YOU COULDN'T BE SAFER ANYWHERE IN THE KINGDOM.
I'D BE SAFER IF I WAS AT HOME...
THE DARKNESS IS MY FRIEND, LITTLE LION. MY FRIEND WOULD NEVER ALLOW HARM TO COME TO YOU WHILE WE'RE HERE.
OH YEAH?... W-W-W-WHAT'S THAT?
THAT, LITTLE LION, IS...

...KING BEAR.
KING BEAR, MEET JOEY, OUR LITTLE LION.
W-WOW! N-NO WONDER THE BEASTIES ARE SC-SCARED OF YOU!
HAHAHA!
AM I THAT FRIGHTENING TO YOUR EYES?
NO, I GUESS NOT...
BEFORE YOU ENTERED, YOU IMAGINED A GIANT MONSTER, SCARIER THAN ANYTHING YOU'D EVER SEEN, DIDN'T YOU?
HOW DID YOU KNOW THAT?
BECAUSE YOU HAVE IMAGINATION. WHAT A STRANGE MAGIC THAT IS. AND LIKE ALL MAGICS, YOU CONTROL IT AS MUCH AS IT CONTROLS YOU.
IT CAN BRING MAGICAL LIFE TO ALL OF YOUR TOYS. IT CAN TURN YOU INTO A GIANT OR ALLOW YOU TO SOAR LIKE AN EAGLE.
BUT WHEN YOU'VE LOST CONTROL OF IT, IT CAN GIVE LIFE TO THOSE THINGS THAT GO BUMP IN THE NIGHT...

I HAVE MAGIC?
YOU HAVE THE ESSENCE OF LIFE, IMAGINATION. THERE IS NO EQUATION, NO FORMULA, NO BLUEPRINT FOR MAKE-BELIEVE. NO STRUCTURE, GUIDELINES OR RULES.
ONLY MAGIC CAN EXIST IN SUCH AN UNFETTERED STATE. ONLY IMAGINATION.
SO, I CAN CONTROL IT? LIKE A WIZARD?
YES, LITTLE LION.
COME WITH ME, AND I'LL SHOW YOU THIS MAGIC YOU CALL IMAGINATION.
OKAY.
TELL ME, LITTLE LION, HAVE YOU EVER FELT YOU WERE BEING WATCHED IN THE DARK?
Y-Y-YES.

THE BEASTIES WATCH YOU FROM THE DARKNESS, JUST AS THEY WATCHED THESE MEMBERS OF THE BEAR GUARD WHO ARE REMEMBERED HERE IN THE HALL OF THE FALLEN.
NO ONE KNOWS WHEN THE BEASTIES FIRST CAME TO LIFE, BUT FROM THE FIRST TIME WE CAME UPON THEM, WE'VE BEEN AT WAR.
TOBIAS BEAR
OUR MISSION WAS CLEAR, TO PROTECT THE CHILDREN. THE PRICE WE PAY FOR THIS MISSION IS OFTEN...
HENRY BEAR
...A DEAR ONE.
HENRY BEAR
WE THOUGHT WE HAD THE UPPER HAND, FOR THE RIVER ROCK ALLOWED US TO KNOW THINGS THAT HAD YET TO HAPPEN.
ONCE THE SACRED STONE WAS LOST, IT WAS ONLY A MATTER OF TIME BEFORE FATE TIPPED THE SCALES AGAINST US...

WITHOUT THE RIVER ROCK, WE'RE NOW AT QUITE THE DISADVANTAGE. WE HAVE TO RELY ON LITTLE BIRDIE'S RECON TO KEEP US INFORMED OF THE BEASTIES' ACTIONS.
BEFORE THE AGENTS OF VALTHRAAX STOLE OUR PRECIOUS STONE, I HAD ONE LAST VISION.
IF THEY SUCCEED WITH THEIR NEWEST PLOT...
...
WE NEED YOUR HELP, LITTLE LION. THE RIVER ROCK HAS SHOWN ME THAT YOU ARE THE KEY.
B-BUT, Y-YOU WERE SUPPOSED TO SEND ME HOME...
YOU PROMISED!
YA WANNA GO HOME, BUT DON'TCHA WANNA BE SAFE WHEN YOU GET THERE?
Y-YES, GRANDMA KEEPS ME SAFE.
WOULDN'T GRANDMA BE PROUD IF YOU KEPT HER SAFE FOR ONCE?
YEAH... BUT, WHAT CAN I DO?

YOU MUST HELP US, JOEY.
WE ARE BORN OF YOUR WORLD. ONLY ONE HUMAN FROM EACH GENERATION CAN FORGE OUR LIFE FORCE. THIS WAS OUR MOST GUARDED SECRET UNTIL THE RIVER ROCK WAS TAKEN FROM US.
NOW THE BEASTIES KNOW OF THE CREATOR...AND MORE IMPORTANTLY, THEY KNOW OF HIS DAUGHTER.
YOUR DESTINY AND HERS ARE INTERTWINED, LITTLE LION.
WHADAYA MEAN 'INNERTWINED'?
YOU ARE SOUL MATES... SHE IS TO BE YOUR WIFE. THIS DESTINY WAS WRITTEN LONG AGO...
WIFE? YUCK!
HEH
HMMM
HEHE
S'NOT FUNNY! I'M NOT MARRYING NO ICKY GIRL!
A WIFE IS ALSO A FRIEND, LITTLE LION.
WOULD YOU WANT YOUR FRIEND TO FALL INTO THE HANDS OF THE BEASTIES?
GOOD FRIENDS ARE HARD TO COME BY, JOEY...
NO...I GUESS NOT.
IF YOU CAN PROTECT ME, I GUESS I CAN HELP YOU PROTECT HER...
THAT'S MY BOY!
NOW LET'S ROLL!

THERE'S LITTLE BIRDIE NOW!
I HOPE HE GOT THE INFORMATION WE NEED...
YOU DON'T SEEM SO NERVOUS NOW, JOEY.
I GUESS I WAS REALLY NERVOUS WHEN WE FIRST GOT HERE...BUT NOW, ALL I CAN THINK ABOUT IS THAT MY GRANDMA ALWAYS GIVES THE BEST PRESENTS.
KING BEAR'S PLAN WILL COME OFF WITHOUT A HITCH. YOU'LL BE A HERO WHEN YOU SEE HER AGAIN.
TIME TO MOVE OUT.
...AND NEVER FORGET THAT CAGE.
WHEN THIS IS OVER, WE'LL FIND THAT CAVE AND MAKE SURE NO ONE IS EVER TRAPPED IN THAT THING AGAIN.
YOU KNOW, YOU'RE THE FIRST LITTLE BOY I'VE EVER SEEN.
WELL, IN REAL LIFE, ANYWAY...
REALLY?
I'M SO SORRY, SIR, WE HAD NO IDEA...
DON'T WORRY, THE LAST TIME I WAS HERE YOU WERE JUST A CUB.
YOU'VE GOT THE PLAN, BIRDIE?
I'LL MEET YOU AT THE GROVE!
GOOD LUCK!
SO, WHAT DID YOU THINK OF THE KING?
HE WAS SUPER COOL! KINDA REMINDED ME OF MY GRANDMA, TOO.

ONCE WE HEAR FROM LITTLE BIRDIE, I'LL MEET YOU AT THE RENDEZVOUS WITH THE BEAR GUARD!
YOUR GRANDMOTHER WILL BE PROUD OF YOU.
SHE'S NOT GOING TO BELIEVE THIS!
ALMOST THERE, I JUST HOPE THOSE BEASTIES BRING SOME COURAGE THIS TIME, I HATE CHASING AFTER THEM.
THEY BROUGHT COURAGE TO THE GREAT BATTLE, NOT THAT IT HELPED THEM.
THEY JUST DIDN'T KNOW HOW TO USE IT.
IF YOU BEAT THEM BEFORE, HOW COME THEY'RE STILL HERE?
LIKE ALL COWARDS, THEY HID AND PLOTTED AND SCHEMED...
AND THEN THE SNEAK ATTACKS AND AMBUSHES BEGAN...
WE BOASTED OF OUR VICTORY, ONLY TO LOSE SO MUCH MORE...
BUT, WE'LL WIN OUT THIS TIME. KING BEAR IS MUCH TOO SMART FOR THEM.
I SURE HOPE SO...

VENUS, MINERVA, STAND GUARD WHILE I OPEN THE PORTAL.
ENE MEENE MYNE...
...MOE!
FWASH
POOF
SLICK!
AFTER YOU...
WHY, THANK YOU...
WELL, THIS WASN'T AS HARD AS I EXPECTED.
SEE, I TOLD YOU THIS WOULD BE...

...EASY.
To Be Continued

LR
05
BAM
"The Mission"
Drawn by Luke Ross
With Colors by Jason Keith

JACK

...UPON A TIME THERE WAS A YOUNG GIRL NAMED...
DAD, I'M ALMOST A TEENAGER NOW, I DON'T NEED YOU TO TELL ME BEDTIME STORIES.
STOP TREATING ME LIKE I'M A LITTLE KID.
COURTNEY, YOU MIGHT BE GROWING UP, BUT YOU'RE NOT GROWN UP YET...
...AND YOU'LL ALWAYS BE MY BEAUTIFUL LITTLE GIRL.
I'LL BE FINE, DAD, JUST LET ME GO TO SLEEP...
OKAY, DEAR, WELL, GOOD NIGHT.
DAAAAAAD!
SMOOCH
I DON'T CARE HOW OLD YOU GET--YOU'LL NEVER BE TOO OLD FOR A GOODNIGHT KISS FROM YOUR FATHER.

I'LL BE DOWN IN THE WORKSHOP IF YOU NEED ME.
GOOD NIGHT, DAAAD.
OH, ORSON, WHEN WILL HE EVER LET ME GROW UP?
ALL RIGHT, MUMBLER, DON'T SCREW IT UP THIS TIME!
YOU SCREWED IT UP LAST TIME!

FOR SUCH A SMALL KID...SHE SURE IS...
...HEAVY.
WHACK
FIRST AID
COME ON, SLACKER!
GET THAT RUNT TIED UP!
I'M HURRYING...
HURRY! THEY'RE GETTING AWAY!
LEAVE THE SHRIMP, MUMBLER, WE GOT THE KID.
WE'RE TOO LATE!
OPEN IT BACK UP, PALLO!
I'M TRYING, MINERVA...BUT IT'LL TAKE A MINUTE...
ORSON, WHAT HAPPENED?
COURTNEY HAD ME PINNED. SHE MUST'VE ROLLED OVER IN HER SLEEP, VENUS.
AHHH, IT HURTS TO TALK...

GOT THE PORTAL OPEN, LET'S ROLL!
NU-UH... WE SHOULD GET HELP! I'M SURE THEY HAVE A PHONE, I CAN CALL MY GRANDMA!
THERE'S NO TIME FOR THAT, JOEY, WE HAVE TO GO BEFORE THEY GET AWAY!
COME, LITTLE LION, WE'RE WASTING TIME!
B-BUT... MY GRANDMA CAN HELP US...
NO ADULT CAN GO TO THE KINGDOM. IT'S UP TO YOU.
REMEMBER WHAT KING BEAR TOLD YOU.
JOEY, WHAT WOULD TIGER-MAN DO?
OKAY, LET'S GO!
I'M NEVER GONNA GET HOME...

WE'RE TOO LATE, THEY'VE GONE INTO THE FOREST.
THEY COULD BE HEADING ANYWHERE IN THE BEASTIE LANDS...
NOW WHAT, PALLO?
I ANTICIPATED THIS...
ROOAARR!

KROAARR!
...NO WAY GROK IS GOING TO LET YOU EAT HER, MUMBLER!
HE MIGHT...
AND, JUST WHAT MAKES YOU THINK THAT?
HE MIGHT BE FULL ALREADY.
AND WHY WOULD HE BE FULL ALREADY?
'CAUSE HE MIGHT EAT YOU WHEN WE GET THERE.
SHUT UP!
HEH.

LITTLE BIRDIE!
LONG TIME NO SEE!
WHAT'S THE WORD?
THE BEASTIES ARE HEADING TOWARDS THE CAVES ON THE OTHER SIDE OF THE HAUNTED FOREST. THEY HAVE COURTNEY WITH THEM. I THINK SHE'S OKAY, BUT I HEARD THEM MENTION GROK.
I KNEW GROK WOULD BE INVOLVED! WE'VE WASTED ENOUGH TIME. 'BIRDIE, HEAD FOR THE CASTLE AND SUMMON THE GUARD TO MEET US AT THE CAVE.
YES, SIR!
COME ON, WE HAVE TO MAKE IT THROUGH THE HAUNTED FOREST AS QUICKLY AS WE CAN TO AVOID THE GHOSTS!
HAUNTED FOREST? NO ONE SAID ANYTHING ABOUT A HAUNTED FOREST!
I DON'T WANNA GO IN THERE...
BAH! GHOSTS CAN'T HURT US...
WELL, I DIDN'T GO INTO THE HAUNTED HOUSE BACK HOME...I GUESS THIS'LL SHOW EVERYONE I'M NOT SCARED OF NO STUPID OLD GHOST!

YOU, LUNK HEAD. HURRY UP, YOU'RE SLOWING ME DOWN.
THOSE STUMPS YOU CALL LEGS ARE WHAT'S SLOWING YOU DOWN, GRUMBLE, NOT ME.
I THOUGHT YOU SAID THIS FOREST WAS HAUNTED. DON'T YOU NEED GHOSTS AND STUFF TO BE HAUNTED?
THEY DON'T BOTHER US. WE BRING THEM FOOD.
AND IF YOU DON'T SHUT UP, YOU'RE GONNA BE THEIR NEXT MEAL.
Y-Y-YEAH, WHATEVER...
LOOKS LIKE WE BEAT THE OTHERS HERE.
ALL RIGHT, GET HER IN THE CAGE, THEN WE JUST HAVE TO WAIT FOR GROK TO GET HERE.
AND THEN HE CAN EAT YOU.
IF YOU SAY THAT ONE MORE TIME...

SO, WHY IS THIS PLACE HAUNTED? DID IT GROW ON SOME SECRET INDIAN BURIAL GROUND OR SOMETHING?
SECRET INDIAN BURIAL GROUND. ALL THE BEST HAUNTED HOUSES ARE BUILT ON THEM, YA KNOW.
SECRET WHATSA-WHO WHAT?
HAVEN'T YOU GUYS EVER SEEN ANY HAUNTED HOUSE MOVIES?
WHAT'S A MOVIE?
THE BEASTIES RETREATED HERE AFTER THE GREAT BATTLE, LITTLE LION. LEGEND TELLS THAT MANY OF THEM WHO WERE WOUNDED IN THE BATTLE DIED HERE.
AND NOW THEIR GHOSTS WANT REVENGE!
FEW WHO ENTER THE FOREST ALONE EVER RETURN...

DON'T FORGET TO LOCK IT. WE DON'T WANT HER GETTING OUT.
THANKS FOR REMINDING ME, I WAS JUST GONNA LEAVE THE DOOR OPEN.
IDIOT...
LET ME OUT OF HERE!
JUST YOU WAIT UNTIL MY DAD FINDS OUT ABOUT THIS!
HOW'S HER DADDY GONNA FIND OUT, GRUMBLE?
IS EVERYONE HERE STUPID BUT ME?! HE WON'T FIND OUT! NO ONE KNOWS WE'RE HERE!
WELL, IF NO ONE KNOWS WE'RE HERE, WHO'S CASTING THAT SHADOW?
UH-OH...
AHHHHHH!!

WHAT'S THAT? IS THAT A GHOST?
NAH, IT'S NOTHING... JUST MY IMAGINATION...
WHEN I WAS A LITTLE GIRL, I WAS VERY AFRAID OF THE DARK...
BECAUSE YOU HAVE IMAGINATION. WHAT A STRANGE MAGIC THAT IS. AND LIKE ALL MAGICS, YOU CONTROL IT AS MUCH AS IT CONTROLS YOU.
BUT WHEN YOU LOSE CONTROL, IT CAN GIVE LIFE TO THOSE THINGS THAT GO BUMP IN THE NIGHT...
HEY, KIDDO, HOW YOU HOLDIN' UP?
ALL RIGHT...
So, how am I the key? How is MY imagination going to save the day? Especially if all I can imagine right now is big, scary monsters?

BUFFOONS! WHAT TOOK YOU SO LONG?
Mmmmmm... SHE LOOKS GOOD ENOUGH TO EAT...
VALTHRAAX WILL BE PLEASED...
G-G-GROK! MY LORD, WE DIDN'T EXPECT YOU SO SOON!
STOP GROVELING! I HATE IT WHEN YOU GROVEL!
DID HE SAY "VALTHRAAX"?
GROVEL SOME MORE, HE LOVES IT WHEN YOU DO THAT.
SILENCE!
I WANT TO GO HOME, I WANT TO GO HOME, I WANT TO GO HOME...

Man, these woods ARE scary. Is that just my imagination, too?
Am I just imagining EVERYTHING?
HOW'S THE KNEE, KIDDO? LOOKS LIKE IT'S HEALED UP A BIT.
IT'S OKAY... I GUESS...
I never imagined PAIN before...
I'M SURPRISED YOU DIDN'T REALLY COMPLAIN ABOUT THAT, IT LOOKS LIKE IT STINGS. IF IT WAS ME, I'D HAVE COMPLAINED, BUT NOT YOU...NOSIRREE.
NO, YOU WOULDN'T HAVE. YOU'RE BIG AND STRO--
LOOK OUT!!!

GHOSTS!

ROOAARR!
RAAARR!!

DON'T LET THEM GET JOEY.
RRRRRRR!
THEY'LL NEVER TOUCH HIM!
REEARRR
YOU PICKED THE WRONG PRIDE TO MESS WITH BEASTIE!
JOEY, GET DOWN BEHIND THAT BUSH, WE'LL TAKE CARE OF THESE CHUMPS IN NO TIME FLAT!
ohmygoshohmygoshohmygosh--

YOU MORONS ARE IN BIG TROUBLE WHEN MY DAD FINDS OUT ABOUT THIS!
YA KNOW, IF VALTHRAAX EATS HER, WE WON'T HAVE TO LISTEN TO HER MOUTH ANYMORE...
AND IF HE EATS YOU, I WON'T HAVE TO LISTEN TO YOUR...
SILENCE!
FOOLS!
YOUR DADDY? SO, ABNER IS STILL ALIVE. HE WOULDN'T BE IF THOSE STUPID STUFFED ANIMALS HADN'T GOTTEN IN THE WAY...
THAT DAY IS BURNED INTO OUR MEMORY...
WHAT DO YOU MEAN?
HOW DO YOU KNOW MY DAD?

RAARRRRRR
GET DOWN HERE AND FIGHT, COWARD!
ANYONE WANT TO PLAY TAG? I'M IT!
I GOTTA HELP... BUT...

YOUR FATHER IGNITED THE GREAT BATTLE!
"WHEN HE LEARNED WE WERE OUT TO GET HIM, HE SENT THE ENTIRE STUFFED ANIMAL MILITIA AFTER US!
"IT WAS THE FIRST TIME OUR ARMIES CLASHED. A DAY THAT SHOULD HAVE MARKED OUR VICTORY!
"BUT THOSE CURSED STUFFED ANIMALS TRICKED US!
"THOSE THREE BLASTED NIGHT PRIDE SQUADS FLANKED US. TOO AFRAID TO FIGHT US HEAD ON...
"WHEN THE BATTLE WAS OVER, WE'D LOST MANY OF OUR FAMILY..."
NOW IT'S TIME FOR ABNER...

"...TO LOSE SOMEONE, TOO..."
THEY CALL ME CRUSH, 'CAUSE THAT'S WHAT I DO TO LITTLE KITTIES WHO WANDER INTO MY FOREST!
AND THESE ARE MY FRIENDS...
...BUMBLE...
...DRIBBLE...
...DROOL...
...AND, MY BROTHER, MUNCH!
MUNCH POUND SILLY KITTY!
HEY! KEEP YOUR HANDS TO YOURSELF! I DON'T DO THAT ON THE FIRST DATE!

CRUSH MAKE KITTY QUIET!
HERE, KITTY, KITTY, KITTY.
GET OFF ME, YOU SLIMEBALL!
HEHEHEHE!
WHACK
AHHH!
YOU SHOULD HAVE AT LEAST TAKEN DANCING LESSONS FIRST, YOU'RE ALL LEFT FEET!
BAD KITTY! NO MORE JOKES!
SMASH
UH-OH...I THINK YOU KILLED HIM...GROK IS NOT GOING TO LIKE THAT...HE WANTED TO KILL THIS ONE HIMSELF.

SHOULD WE LEAVE HIM HERE, CRUSH?
NO. WE TAKE HIM TO GROK. WE CAN JUST SAY WE DIDN'T KNOW HE WAS DEAD.
TH-THEY K-KILLED ARES?!
THEY KILLED HIM! OHMYGOSH! THEY KILLED HIM!
WHAT AM I GOING TO DO NOW?
To Be Continued

"My Hero"
Drawn by Todd Nauck
with Colors by Jack Lawrence

Lions, Tigers and Bears

BE BRAVE, JOSEPH...
BE BRAVE, LITTLE LION...
I CAN'T... I CAN'T HELP MY FRIENDS...I CAN'T BE BRAVE WITH ARES DEAD...

HA! THE NIGHT PRIDE'S NOT SO TOUGH AFTER ALL!
I-I-I T-TOLD Y-YOU S-S-SO, C-C-CRUSH.
CRUSH! MUNCH! LORD VALTHRAAX WILL BE PLEASED THAT YOU'VE CAPTURED THE NIGHT PRIDE.
SORRY, GROK. IF IT WASN'T FOR MUMBLER HERE, I COULD'VE CAUGHT THEM MYSELF.
AND IF IT WEREN'T FOR YOU, GRUMBLE, I'D HAVE BEEN AN ONLY CHILD...
...A HAPPY, ONLY CHILD.
I GOT YOUR "ONLY CHILD" RIGHT HERE...
SILENCE! INCOMPETENT FOOLS!
MUNCH, BUMBLER, PUT THE OTHERS BY THE CAGE.
WHAT SHOULD DROOL AND I DO WITH ARES, BOSS?
HE'S OBVIOUSLY DEAD, PUT HIM WITH THE FEMALES...
...LORD VALTHRAAX MIGHT WANT TO STUFF HIM AS A TROPHY.

PSST, MINERVA, CAN YOU TELL IF ARES IS ALIVE?
I CAN'T SEE HIM...
WHAT DO YOU THINK HAPPENED TO JOEY?
DID MY DAD SEND YOU TO SAVE ME?
WE WERE SENT FOR YOU, COURTNEY... I DON'T KNOW ABOUT THE "SAVE YOU" PART, THOUGH...
...MAYBE NEXT TIME?
HONESTLY, MINERVA, CAN YOU EVER BE SERIOUS?
KING BEAR SENT US TO PROTECT YOU FROM THE BEASTIES. UNFORTUNATELY, WE ARRIVED A FEW SECONDS TOO LATE.
WE'VE BEEN FOLLOWING YOU EVER SINCE THE BEASTIES BROUGHT YOU BACK TO THE KINGDOM.
AT LEAST WE MANAGED TO SAVE ONE KID... FOR ALL THE GOOD IT'S DONE US...

What am I going to do? I have to think of something. King Bear said my imagination was the key...
Maybe I can just try really hard to imagine everything is okay...
EVERY.
THING.
IS.
FINE.
Well...
...THAT didn't work...
...now what?
Maybe...
If I could shoot a GIANT BOULDER at them and then skate in and SAVE THE PRIDE...
JOEY
BEASTIES SUCK
No...that's DUMB.
What am I gonna do?

MAYBE if I...
JOEY
OW!
...awww, who am I kidding...
...I'll never save ANYONE.
Stupid imagination...
Ares would know what to do...
...he'd just STORM THAT CAVE and...
...hey...what's THAT?
WAIT A MINUTE! THAT'S NO GHOST! THAT'S JUST A SCARECROW!
THOSE BEASTIES USED MY IMAGINATION AGAINST ME!
NOW I KNOW WHAT KING BEAR WAS TALKING ABOUT...

SO, THIS IS THE HELP YOUR DADDY SENT? IT LOOKS LIKE HE DIDN'T CARE ENOUGH FOR YOU TO ACTUALLY SAVE YOU.
DON'T LISTEN TO HIM, COURTNEY. YOUR FATHER LOVES YOU VERY MUCH.
OH, WE'RE NOT DONE SAVING HER YET. WE'LL DO IT ON OUR SCHEDULE, NOT YOURS, RAT-FACE.
I'D THINK YOU'RE BRAVE... IF YOU WEREN'T SO STUPID, MINERVA...
AND I'D THINK YOU'D INVEST IN SOME MOUTHWASH...
YOU LEAVE THEM ALONE, YA BIG STUPID-HEAD!
OH, HOW COURAGEOUS!
YOU WON'T BE SO VALIANT ONCE YOU ACCEPT THE FACT THAT NO ONE CAN HELP YOU NOW.

WE'LL FIND OUT HOW SMART THOSE BEASTIES ARE WHEN THEY SEE *THIS*...
NOW IF I CAN TIME THIS *JUST* RIGHT...
I SURE HOPE THIS WORKS...
HERE GOES NOTHIN'.

THIS IS THE POLICE! COME OUT WITH YOUR HANDS UP!
GRUMBLE, CRUSH, TAKE THE OTHERS AND SEE WHAT'S GOING ON OUT THERE!

BRRRRRRAAR!
IT'S THE STUPID BEAR GUARD! NOW'S OUR CHANCE FOR REVENGE!
GET THEM!
RRRRAAH!
IT SOUNDS LIKE MY DAD CALLED THE COPS ON YOU, FISH BREATH!
GRRRR...
I THINK OUR LITTLE LION LEARNED TO BE BRAVE.
LOOKS LIKE THAT'S ALL OF THEM.
NOW'S MY CHANCE...

ARES CAN'T BE DEAD...
...HE MUST JUST BE SLEEPING...
...STUFFED ANIMALS CAN'T DIE...
...CAN THEY?
LOOK OUT, KID!
AND JUST WHERE DO YOU THINK YOU'RE GOING, RUNT?
AAAAH!!
COME ON, BIG GUY, WAKE UP!
PLEASE WAKE UP...
I CAN'T DO THIS WITHOUT YOU...

HAHAHAHAHAHA!!
IT'S JUST LIKE KING BEAR TO SEND A BABY TO DO A MAN'S JOB.
IT'S ALL OVER BUT THE CRYING NOW...
=PFFT= PITIFUL...
WHAT'S KEEPING THOSE IMBECILES?
ARES, WHY WON'T YOU WAKE UP?
I FEAR OUR FRIEND IS TRULY DEAD, LITTLE LION...
NO.
NO! HE CAN'T BE!
WAKE UP!

NOOOO...

HEY... KIDDO...
I KNEW YOU WERE JUST SLEEPING! I KNEW IT!
WHERE ARE WE?
MY HEAD HURTS...
SO WHAT'S THE PLAN, BIG GUY? WHAT DO WE HAVE TO DO TO GET OUT OF HERE?
IT'S STILL UP TO YOU, JOEY. YOU HAVE TO SAVE US.
YOU HAVE TO SAVE COURTNEY.
BUT...HOW?
JOEY, YOU JUST HAVE TO BE BRAVE...

YOUR IDEA OF BEING BRAVE IS TO TRICK US WITH FAKE BEARS, BOY?!
I THINK THE BOSS IS GONNA KILL 'IM!
HE WOULDN'T...
BOSS, YA CAN'T KILL 'IM! NOT UNTIL LORD VALTHRAAX GETS HERE.
UNHAND ME, FOOL!
LORD VALTHRAAX WON'T BE HERE FOR HOURS, SO IT LOOKS LIKE HE'LL JUST HAVE TO SIT THIS ONE OUT...
I THINK OUR VISITORS ARE ABOUT TO HAVE AN ACCIDENT...

YOUR IMAGINATION WILL SAVE US...
I'VE HAD ENOUGH OF YOU, MEAN OLD BEASTIES! IF YOU THINK YOU'RE GOING TO HURT MY FRIENDS, YOU'D BETTER THINK AGAIN!
IT'S GOING TO TAKE A LOT MORE THAN A SAD LITTLE BOY WHO THINKS HE'S FOUND SOME COURAGE TO STOP US THIS TIME.
SHINCK
SHUUNCK

I BELIEVE YOU'RE *RIGHT*...
BEASTIES, I'D LIKE YOU TO MEET *TOBIAS* AND *HENRY.* THEY'RE HEROES OF THE *GREAT BATTLE*...
...AND MY *IMAGINARY FRIENDS.*

MORE PARLOR TRICKS! GET THEM!
I CAN IMAGINE AS MANY BEARS AS I WANT, AND YOU'D BETTER BELIEVE THEY'RE REAL ENOUGH TO STOP YOU!
FORGET THE KID-- GET THE GIRL!
SHE'S THE KEY!
WITHOUT HER THERE WON'T BE ANY MORE STUFFED ANIMALS!
YOU HEARD THE BOSS, GET THE GIRL!

STOP THEM!
B-B... B-B-BOSS?!
RARR!
OOOOOOF!
CRAAAAK
CAVE IN!
RUN!

ALRIGHT, LET'S GET OUT OF HERE!
SNAPT
COME ON, COURTNEY! RUN!
HURRY!!
I'LL GET YOU, KID, YOU'LL NEVER SLEEP AGAIN!

RRRMMMBBBLLL
IS EVERYONE ALL RIGHT?
EVERYONE EXCEPT THOSE BEASTIES.
YOU CAN LET GO NOW.
OH... YEAH... RIGHT.
SORRY.
WELL, WELL...
...IT LOOKS LIKE YOU REALLY DIDN'T NEED OUR HELP AS MUCH AS YOU THOUGHT!
AFTER ALL THESE YEARS, IT'S GOOD TO KNOW THE CAVE WAS FINALLY DESTROYED.
HINTO, I'D LIKE YOU TO MEET JOEY.
JOEY, THIS IS GENERAL HINTO, ONE OF KING BEAR'S ADVISORS.
NICE TO MEET YOU, SIR.
KING BEAR KNEW YOU'D UNLOCK THE SECRET OF THE IMAGINARY BEARS, JOEY...
WELL, WE BETTER GET YOU TWO BACK TO THE CRYSTAL CASTLE, KING BEAR IS EXPECTING US.

...FOR YOUR SERVICES TO THE KINGDOM...
...AND BRAVERY IN THE FACE OF DANGER.
HOORAY!!
PALLO, I THINK IT'S TIME YOU TOOK THESE LITTLE ONES HOME.
HOME? DO WE HAVE TO?
I'M AFRAID SO, LITTLE LION, BUT, I'M SURE WE'LL MEET AGAIN SOON...

WAIT UNTIL GRANDMA HEARS ABOUT *THIS!*
SHE ALREADY KNOWS ABOUT US, LITTLE LION. HAVE YOU NEVER NOTICED WHO *HER* STUFFED ANIMAL IS?
YOU MEAN THE *BEAR*...
...WITH THE *ROBE*...
...AND *CROWN*...?
YOU'RE JUST FIGURING THIS OUT NOW?
WELL, I'VE BEEN BUSY...

I GUESS IT DOES FEEL PRETTY GOOD TO BE HOME, HUH, COURTNEY?
AND NOW THAT I KNOW YOU LIVE JUST A BLOCK AWAY FROM MY NEW HOUSE, I GUESS WE'LL BE SEEING EACH OTHER MORE OFTEN...
WE'D BETTER...
AH, YOUNG LOVE...
S'NOT LOVE!
SMOOCH
...
SEE YOU SOON!
BYE, MY LITTLE LION.
TIME TO GET YOU HOME, JOEY.
TOLD YA.

WE'LL GET YOU YET, KID!
GRRRRRRR...

WHAZAT?
MUST HAVE BEEN A DREAM...
The End

"Joey and Company"
By Derrick Fish

Joey and Courtney thought they were safe from us after the events at the cave. But as this next story will show you, they'll never be safe from the Beasties!

A few months after our first meeting, Joey's aunt invited him to come to Phoenix and visit her for the weekend. After some whining, Joey was able to get his mother and Courtney's father, Abner to let that little trouble maker join him. So they put the kids on the plane and sent them to Phoenix.

But they put the stuffed animals in the suitcase, heh. First mistake.

Airline luggage spends a lot of time in the dark... and it's easy for things to get lost in the dark.

The dark is my favorite place to be because there's nothing I love more than watching kids get scared!

All you have to do is wait for the right moment, make sure the closet door creaks when you open it and cast some really spooky shadows on the walls. Their eyes get all bugged out, their jaws flop open and then their imagination does the rest!

I love it!

The part I love the most is when we jump out of the closet. Maybe it's the screams, maybe it's the looks of sheer terror. Whatever it is, I wouldn't trade it for anything!

If I could only get that shrimp Grumble to let me go first, it'd be perfect.

Anyway...

We jumped out right on time, the kids were terrified!

And to top it off, those stupid stuffed animals were still trapped in that suitcase!

This night was going perfectly...

At least until the kid hit his head...

I felt like I had a charlie horse in my stomach when we were trapped in that suitcase!

I knew something was wrong. I just knew it, don't ask me how.

We got out a second too late, but that wasn't going to stop me from hunting those Beasties to the end of the Kingdom and beyond.

I mean come on, just how many places can a giant orange set of teeth and a fuzzy grape hide anyway?

Those Beasties just don't know what they're up against. We've proven our military superiority over them time and again!

While they may have thought they escaped, there was no way I was going to let a little thing like the Haunted Forest stop me from getting Courtney back!

I've sworn an oath to protect her and no matter how far I had to track them, nothing was going to stop me from saving her!

I really wish those Beasties would just give up trying to rule the world.

The Kingdom is such a beautiful place, if they'd only take the time to see that, I bet they'd be much happier.

I mean, life is meant to be enjoyed, not to waste in angry pursuits and evil deeds, ya know.

I really wonder why they just can't seem to realize that.

Well, whatever their mental malfunction is, there's no way I'm going to stand for them messing with our kids!

I was so glad when Orson, Ares & Venus came out of the woods! There's nothing worse than being carried around by a smelly old beastie, then tied to a tree, then picked up again by the same smelly, old Beastie!

He smells like sweat socks mixed with cat litter!

YUCK!

There's no reason why anyone should be that smelly!

Maybe that's why the Beasties are always mean...

I'd be mean if I never had any friends, and you just can't make friends when you're that stinky.

I guess there are times when you can be too brave.

Times where you think you're so brave that you do stupid stuff... like leave your stuffed animals in a suitcase and let the Beasties capture you.

But I guess I'd rather be brave enough to face those stupid Beasties now, instead of goin' back to being scared all the time...

Even if it doesn't always work out the way I imagine it will.

While I cannot recall the countless names of Stuffed Animals who have given their lives to protect children down through the ages, there are two I could not forget no matter how hard I might try.

Henry and Tobias Bear lived the lives of heroes. Their triumphs were legendary, their sacrifices undeniable.

Even now that they've gone beyond the veil of the living, they still return to protect the lives of little ones.

I remember my Grandmother fondly. She was always quick with a smile and had many entertaining stories to tell about the overabundance of stuffed animals around her house.

One day, while I was pretending to be a Flying Ace, I stumbled into her workshop, where she was teaching my father to make these animals.

I found it all rather boring at first, until I learned that these were more than just toys... they were mythical creatures from a magical world. A magic made of the same energy that makes us smile, laugh and love.

This magic has been passed down from generation to generation.

Help keep the magic alive!

"Courtney and Orson"
By
Theo Bain

"Cornered"
By
Jack Lawrence

"Snowy Wastes"
By Jack Lawrence
JACK